BONE SPEARS AND STARSHIPS

Voyagers of the Galileo

First edition

This book was professionally typeset on Reedsy.
Find out more at reedsy.com

Contents

Chapter 1

Voyagers of the Galileo

Captain Nathaniel Ford leaned back in his chair on the bridge of the Galileo, skimming through the latest mission reports displayed on his data pad. The monotonous list of routine scans and minor anomalies had become all too familiar. He glanced up at Lieutenant Jess Hayes, who stood beside him, her posture rigid and her eyes fixed on her own data pad.

"Anything noteworthy, Jess?" Ford asked, his voice authoritative yet carrying a hint of frustration. Jess shook her head, her auburn hair swaying slightly.

"Nothing significant, Captain," she replied, her tone cautious and detail-oriented as always. "Just more of the same—minor energy fluctuations, debris fields, and routine system checks. No sign of anything particularly interesting."

Ford sighed, setting the data pad aside. He rubbed his temples, feeling the weight of monotony pressing down on him. "We've been out here for months, Jess. Routine scans, minor anomalies... it's all just so mundane. I signed up for this to make a difference, to find something that matters."

Jess glanced at him, her green eyes filled with concern. "I understand, Captain. But we have to stay cautious. Space is vast, and not every mission is going to be groundbreaking. We have a duty to the crew's safety first and foremost." Her voice was steady, but Ford could sense the underlying tension between her caution and his yearning for adventure.

In the background, the sound of clanging tools echoed through the bridge as Engineer Maria "Ria" Lopez worked energetically on a piece of equipment. Her short black hair was pulled back, and she wore a look of intense concentration. "Ugh, I swear, if I have to recalibrate one more plasma conduit, I might lose my mind," she muttered, her voice carrying a mix of frustration and enthusiasm.

Dr. Samuel "Sam" Patel entered the bridge, his warm brown eyes scanning the room. He approached Captain Ford, holding a medical scanner in one hand. "Captain, just doing my rounds," he said, his voice warm and compassionate. He glanced at the crew, noticing their sluggish movements and lackluster expressions. "I've been observing some signs of boredom and restlessness among the crew. It's not just the equipment that needs a bit of excitement."

Pilot Ethan "Ace" Morgan lounged casually at his station, a smirk playing on his lips as he overheard the conversation. "Well, maybe if we could find something a bit more thrilling than space dust, we wouldn't be so bored," he quipped, his voice laid-back and cocky. "I'd kill for a bit of excitement right about now. All this routine flying is putting me to sleep."

Communications Officer Lana Mitchell, her long black hair falling neatly over her shoulders, suddenly straightened in her seat. Her fingers flew over the console as she adjusted the settings. "Captain, I'm picking up some unusual signals," she said, her voice diplomatic and articulate. "It's faint, but definitely there. It's not like anything we've encountered before."

Ford's eyes lit up with interest as he turned his attention to Lana. "Can you pinpoint the source?" he asked, a spark of anticipation in his authoritative tone. Lana nodded, her blue eyes focused on the screen. "It's coming from a nearby sector, about a day's travel from our current location. It might be worth investigating."

***

Captain Nathaniel Ford stood on the bridge of the Galileo, his eyes scanning the star-studded expanse visible through the large view port. He was deep in thought, considering the crew's recent conversations about their monotonous routine, when Lana Mitchell's voice broke through the silence. "Captain, I'm detecting an unusual energy reading from a nearby sector," she said, her tone professional yet tinged with curiosity.

Ford's interest was immediately piqued. He turned toward Lana, his eyes narrowing with focus. "What kind of energy reading, Lana?" he asked, his authoritative voice cutting through the quiet hum of the bridge. He took a few steps toward her station, eager to see the data for himself.

Before Lana could respond, Lieutenant Jess Hayes stepped forward, her expression cautious. "Captain, we should consider the risks," she interjected, her green eyes reflecting her concern. "An unknown energy reading could mean anything—from natural phenomena to potential threats. We can't afford to put the crew in unnecessary danger."

Ford glanced at Jess, his expression a mix of determination and impatience. "I understand the risks, Jess, but we've been out here for months with nothing but routine scans and minor anomalies. This could be something significant, something that gives our mission purpose," he argued, his voice firm. "We can't keep playing it safe forever."

Jess crossed her arms, standing her ground. "Our primary duty is to ensure the safety of the crew. We need more information before diving headfirst into the unknown. We should analyze the data thoroughly and proceed with caution," she countered, her tone steady and unwavering.

Ford took a deep breath, weighing Jess's concerns against his own drive for a meaningful mission. He looked around at the bridge, at his crew who were capable and ready. "We'll proceed, but with caution," he finally declared, his voice resolute. "Lana, I want a full analysis of that energy reading. Jess, prepare the crew for potential hazards. We're going to investigate."

***

Captain Nathaniel Ford stood at the head of the table in the common area, his gaze sweeping over the gathered crew. The room was filled with a palpable tension as Lieutenant Jess Hayes stepped forward, her expression serious. "Captain, I have to voice my concerns about exploring the Forsaken Fleet," she began, her tone cautious and measured. "We have no idea what we're walking into. There could be any number of threats waiting for us—unstable structures, dormant defense systems, even hostile forces."

Ford watched Jess as she spoke, her green eyes reflecting her deep worry. He appreciated her thoroughness and commitment

4

to the crew's safety, even if her cautious nature often clashed with his own desire for adventure. "We need to consider the potential risks carefully," she continued, "and ensure we have contingency plans in place for every possible scenario."

Before Jess could elaborate further, Ace Morgan leaned back in his chair, a playful smirk on his face. "Oh, come on, Jess," he said, his voice laid-back and dismissive. "We've faced plenty of unknowns before. What's the point of being out here if we don't take a few risks? The Forsaken Fleet sounds like exactly the kind of adventure we signed up for."

Dr. Sam Patel, who had been listening quietly, leaned forward with a thoughtful expression. "Ace, Jess has a point," he said, his voice warm and compassionate. "We need to think about the potential health risks, too. Ancient ships could have unstable environments, lingering pathogens, or radiation leaks. We can't afford to overlook these dangers."

Ria Lopez, who had been fidgeting with a small device, finally spoke up, her eyes alight with excitement. "But think about the technological advancements we could uncover!" she argued, her voice energetic and informal. "The Forsaken Fleet could hold advanced tech that could revolutionize our systems. This is a once-in-a-lifetime opportunity to find something truly groundbreaking."

Captain Ford listened intently to each of his crew members, weighing their points carefully. Jess's caution, Sam's health concerns, Ace's thrill-seeking, and Ria's enthusiasm for technological discovery all swirled in his mind. He appreciated their perspectives, knowing that their varied viewpoints made the team stronger. Finally, he straightened up and made his decision. "We're going to investigate," he said decisively. "But we'll do it with all necessary precautions. Jess, draft contingency plans. Sam, prepare medical protocols. Ria, ready the engineering team. Ace, plot a safe course. We move forward together, as a team."

***

Captain Nathaniel Ford stood on the bridge of the Galileo, the usual hum of the ship's systems a comforting backdrop to his thoughts. Suddenly, a chime echoed through the room, signaling an incoming transmission. Ford glanced at the holographic projector, watching as it flickered to life. "Captain, we're receiving a transmission," Lana Mitchell announced from her station, her fingers dancing over the controls. "It's from Dr. Elara Winters."

The hologram stabilized, revealing Dr. Elara Winters—a woman with intense eyes and a wild mane of graying hair. Her image wavered slightly, but her voice came through clear and sharp. "Captain Ford, my name is Dr. Elara Winters," she began, her tone carrying a hint of manic energy. "I've been studying the Forsaken Fleet for years. I can offer you invaluable expertise and insights in exchange for passage aboard the Galileo. Trust me, you'll need my knowledge to navigate the dangers ahead."

Dr. Winters's holographic form leaned forward, her eyes gleaming with fervor. "The Forsaken Fleet is a treasure trove of advanced technology," she said, her voice rising with excitement. "I've identified ships with capabilities far beyond anything currently known. Weapons, propulsion systems, even medical advancements that could revolutionize our understanding. But it's also riddled with dangers—automated defenses, unstable power sources, and remnants of whatever ancient war left them derelict."

6

Captain Ford watched Dr. Winters closely, his mind racing. Her knowledge could indeed be invaluable, but her intense demeanor and ethical ambiguity were concerning. "Dr. Winters," he said carefully, his authoritative tone masking his internal conflict, "while your expertise is impressive, your enthusiasm borders on obsession. We need to ensure the safety and well-being of our crew. Can you guarantee that your presence will help us without putting us at unnecessary risk?"

Dr. Winters's intense gaze softened slightly, her determination unwavering. "Captain, I assure you, my knowledge will be crucial to navigating the Forsaken Fleet. I understand the risks, but I also see the potential rewards. Together, we can uncover secrets that have been lost for centuries." Ford took a deep breath, still feeling the weight of his decision. "Alright, Dr. Winters, you have a deal," he said finally. "But remember, the safety of my crew comes first. Welcome aboard the Galileo."

Chapter 2

Captain Nathaniel Ford stood at the helm of the Galileo, eyes
fixed on the view through the massive front view port. The
Forsaken Fleet loomed ahead, a sprawling graveyard of derelict
ships drifting in the void. The sight was both awe-inspiring
and unsettling, a testament to a long-forgotten war that had
left these hulking remnants scattered across space.

Ford's mind raced with the possibilities and dangers
that lay ahead. The eerie stillness of the abandoned
vessels contrasted sharply with the anticipation buzzing
through his crew. Each ship represented a mystery to be solved,
a potential treasure trove of advanced technology or a deadly
trap. He could feel the weight of his decision to explore this
place, but the potential rewards were too significant to ignore.

Ace Morgan took the helm with a confident grin, his hands
moving deftly over the controls. "Alright, let's see what we've
got here," he murmured, more to himself than anyone else. The
Galileo responded smoothly to his touch, weaving through the
labyrinth of twisted metal and forgotten ships. Ace's skill was
undeniable, but there was a recklessness in the way he threaded
the ship through narrow gaps, pushing the limits just for the
thrill of it.

At her station, Ria Lopez's eyes were glued to her console,

her fingers flying over the controls as she conducted detailed scans of the derelict ships. Her face lit up with excitement as the sensors pinged with potential finds. "Captain, we're detecting multiple energy signatures. Some of these ships still have active power sources. There could be some seriously advanced tech out there," she said, her voice brimming with enthusiasm.

Lana Mitchell, seated at the communications console, maintained a steady link with Dr. Elara Winters. "Dr. Winters, we're approaching the first cluster of ships. Any specifics we should be aware of?" she asked, her voice calm and professional. Winters's voice crackled through the comms, intense and slightly unhinged. "Yes, Lana, focus on the larger vessels—they're likely to house the most advanced systems. Be wary of automated defenses; they're still operational in some cases."

Captain Ford and Lieutenant Jess Hayes stood side by side at the tactical station, reviewing the data streaming in from Ria and Lana. Jess pointed to a cluster of ships on the display. "These vessels look like they were heavily armed. If any defenses are still active, that's where they'll be," she said, her voice steady but cautious.

Ford nodded, appreciating Jess's detailed assessment. "We'll approach slowly and scan for any active defenses before we get too close. Ria, prioritize those energy signatures and identify anything we can safely salvage. Ace, keep us steady and be ready to pull back if things get dicey," he commanded, his voice firm and confident. "Let's proceed with caution, but stay alert for opportunities."

***

Captain Nathaniel Ford led his crew through the dimly lit

corridors of the derelict ship, his senses on high alert. The air was thick with dust and the hum of ancient machinery. Suddenly, a sharp click echoed through the hallway, and Ford instinctively halted, raising a hand to signal the others to stop. "Watch your step," he warned, his voice low and controlled. "We've got traps."

Engineer Ria Lopez moved to the front, her eyes scanning the ground and walls for signs of danger. "I see it," she muttered, her voice filled with a mix of excitement and concentration. She knelt down, pulling out a toolkit and deftly disarming the hidden mechanism. Further ahead, a malfunctioning AI drone sputtered to life, its sensors flaring erratically. Ria quickly accessed a nearby terminal, her fingers flying over the keys to reroute the AI's protocols. "That should do it," she said, standing up with a satisfied grin.

As the crew proceeded deeper into the ship, a malfunctioning door suddenly slid shut, catching one of the crew members on the arm. "Ah, damn it!" the crew member exclaimed, clutching their arm in pain. Dr. Sam Patel was at their side in an instant, his medical kit already open. "Hold still," Sam instructed, his voice calm and reassuring. He quickly assessed the injury, cleaning and bandaging the wound with practiced efficiency.

As they advanced through the labyrinthine corridors, the crew turned a corner and found themselves face-to-face with a group of heavily armed mercenaries. Captain Ford's eyes locked onto the leader, a tall, muscular woman with a scar across her cheek and a determined expression. "Captain Lysa Graves," she introduced herself, her voice gruff and commanding. Her hand hovered near her weapon, and her team mirrored her tense stance.

Before anyone could speak, a malfunctioning drone nearby

sparked violently, triggering an immediate reaction from both groups. Ace Morgan sprang into action, his movements quick and precise as he disarmed a mercenary aiming at their group. Jess Hayes, her tactical mind sharp, barked orders to the crew, positioning them defensively and minimizing their exposure. Shots rang out, but the skirmish was brief, ending as quickly as it had begun.

Captain Ford stepped forward, his authoritative presence commanding attention. "Hold your fire!" he shouted, his voice cutting through the tension. The crew and mercenaries lowered their weapons slightly, eyes still wary. Ford addressed Captain Graves directly, his tone firm but diplomatic. "We're here for the same reason—to explore the Forsaken Fleet and uncover its secrets. There's no need for us to be at each other's throats. We can achieve more if we work together."

Graves eyed Ford skeptically, her hand still hovering near her weapon. After a moment of tense silence, she nodded. "Alright, Ford. An uneasy alliance, then. But don't think for a second that I trust you or your crew." Ford inclined his head, acknowledging her terms. "Understood. We'll proceed with caution and respect. Let's see what we can uncover."

***

Captain Nathaniel Ford led his crew deeper into the labyrinthine corridors of the Forsaken Fleet, his gaze sweeping over the remnants of once-mighty star ships. The atmosphere was thick with anticipation and the faint hum of ancient technology. Ria Lopez, at her station, suddenly exclaimed, "Captain, I've picked up a massive energy signature ahead." Ford's pulse quickened at her words, his curiosity piqued by the possibilities lurking in the darkness.

He approached Ria's station, his eyes narrowing as he studied the readouts on her console. "What have you found, Ria?" he asked, his voice steady yet filled with an undercurrent of excitement. Ria looked up at him, her eyes alight with a mixture of awe and determination. "It's the AI-driven battleship V.A.L.O.R., Captain," she replied, her voice barely containing her enthusiasm. "It seems to be still operational."

Dr. Sam Patel joined Captain Ford and Ria at the station, his brow furrowed as he examined the data streaming across the screen. "This isn't just any battleship, Captain," Sam said, his voice tinged with concern. "V.A.L.O.R. was known for its advanced AI systems and formidable weaponry. If it's still operational, we could be dealing with a significant threat."

Before Captain Ford could formulate a response to Sam's warning, the ship's intercom crackled to life with a chilling announcement: "Captain Ford and crew, this is Lieutenant Xander Kane. Stand down and surrender control of V.A.L.O.R. to me, or face the consequences." Ford's jaw clenched as he recognized the cold, manipulative voice of Kane, their supposed ally.

Jess Hayes sprang into action, her mind racing through tactical scenarios as she assessed the sudden threat posed by Kane and his operatives. "Take cover!" she shouted, her voice cutting through the chaos as she directed the crew to strategic positions. With precise commands, she coordinated their defense, aiming to neutralize the immediate danger posed by Kane's ambush.

Amidst the chaos, Captain Ford stepped forward, his voice commanding and steady. "Listen up, everyone! We've faced worse and come out on top," he shouted, rallying his crew. "Ria, keep working on that AI. Sam, stay ready for casualties. Lana, I need you to crack those codes and get us control over V.A.L.O.R. Ace, hold the line and make sure Kane's men don't breach our position."

The crew responded to Ford's authoritative presence, each member falling into their roles with renewed determination. Ria focused on her console, her hands flying over the keys as she delved deeper into V.A.L.O.R.'s systems. Sam readied his medical kit, prepared to handle any injuries that might occur. Lana worked furiously to decode the AI's communications, her brow furrowed in concentration. Ace stood guard, his stance firm and ready to repel any further attacks.

Lana Mitchell's fingers flew over the console as she worked to decode the AI's communications, her eyes darting between lines of encrypted data. "Come on, come on," she muttered under her breath, her concentration unwavering despite the chaos around her. Suddenly, her screen flashed, and she looked up, eyes bright with triumph. "Captain, I've managed to access V.A.L.O.R. 's systems. We might be able to shut it down from here or even take control!"

***

Captain Nathaniel Ford braced himself as the corridor erupted into chaos. Blaster fire and shouts filled the air, echoing off the metallic walls of V.A.L.O.R. The enemy's relentless assault pressed the crew of the **Galileo** back momentarily. Ford's heart pounded, but his mind remained sharp, evaluating the rapidly changing situation.

Ford quickly scanned the battlefield, noting the positions of his crew and the advancing mercenaries. He could see Lieutenant Kane's operatives moving with calculated precision, their cold efficiency evident in their every move. The ferocity of the ambush required immediate and decisive action. "Hold the line!" he shouted, rallying his crew and preparing them for the next phase of the fight.

Amidst the chaos, Captain Ford recognized an opportunity. "We need to take out the AI core!" he commanded, determination etched in his voice. Selecting a small team, including Ace and Ria, he charged forward, weaving through the hail of blaster fire. His bravery inspired the crew, each member pushing their limits to follow his lead.

Ford led the way, his focus unwavering as they made their way deeper into V.A.L.O.R.'s heart. His mind raced with the potential outcomes of their mission—both the dangers and the rewards. Every step brought them closer to the AI core, and every move was a testament to his decisiveness and commitment to the mission's success.

While Ford led the assault, Jess Hayes stayed behind to coordinate the crew's defense. She quickly assessed their positions and identified strategic points to hold off the mercenaries. "Ria, take cover behind that console! Sam, keep an eye on the injured and stay ready for evac!" she barked, her voice clear and commanding.

Engineer Ria Lopez moved swiftly, her hands deftly deactivating traps and rerouting power as they advanced. Beside her, Dr. Sam Patel stayed vigilant, ready to provide medical aid. When a nearby explosion sent debris flying, Sam quickly bandaged a crew member's arm, his calm efficiency ensuring they stayed in the fight. "Keep moving, Ria! I've got this!" he urged.

Ace Morgan, positioned at a strategic point, executed a series of daring maneuvers to create openings for Ford's team. He ducked and rolled, narrowly avoiding enemy fire, and returned shots with precision. "Over here, you tin-cans!" he taunted, drawing fire away from his crew. His reckless bravery paid off as he managed to disrupt the mercenaries' formation.

Lana Mitchell worked furiously at her console, her eyes scanning lines of code as she attempted to shut down V.A.L.O.R.'s communications. Sweat beaded on her forehead, but her hands remained steady. "Almost there... Come on," she muttered. Suddenly, her screen flashes green. "Captain, I've accessed V.A.L.O.R. systems! We might be able to shut it down or even take control!"

Lieutenant Kane, observing the tide turning against his forces, barked orders with a cold, calculated fury. "Deploy the heavy drones and force them back!" he commanded, his voice a chilling contrast to the chaos. His mercenaries responded with precision, deploying advanced combat drones that intensified the assault on the Galileo's crew.

Chapter 3

Captain Nathaniel Ford led his crew into the dimly lit core of V.A.L.O.R., the heart of the massive AI-driven battleship. The hum of dormant machinery surrounded them, and Ford's eyes scanned the room, taking in the complex web of circuits and control panels. "Lana, focus on the central processor," he ordered, his voice steady despite the tension that gripped him.

L ana Mitchell stepped forward, her fingers dancing over the console as she worked quickly to shut down the AI's primary systems. The room seemed to hold its breath, the crew watching intently as she navigated the intricate code. Moments later, the core's lights flickered off, and a silence fell over the room. "It's done," Lana said, her voice breaking the quiet. Ford felt a wave of relief wash over him as the immediate threat was neutralized.

With V.A.L.O.R. deactivated, Captain Ford wasted no time. He began examining the core, his eyes scanning the sophisticated technology. "Ria, over here," he called, beckoning the engineer to his side. Together, they carefully extracted advanced modules and data drives, the fruits of their daring mission.

As they worked, Jess Hayes and Dr. Sam Patel stood a few steps back, their faces thoughtful. "Shutting down an AI like this... it feels like playing god," Jess murmured, her voice filled with unease. Sam nodded, his expression somber. "And we have to ensure this technology is used responsibly. The power here is immense, and it can easily be abused."

Captain Ford looked around at his crew, feeling a surge of pride and gratitude. "We couldn't have done this without each one of you," he said, his voice filled with sincerity. "Ria, your technical expertise; Sam, your unwavering support; Lana, your brilliance; Jess, your tactical mind; and Ace, your daring spirit. We are stronger together, and today we proved it."

***

Captain Nathaniel Ford stood on the bridge of the Galileo, watching as his crew made their final preparations to leave the Forsaken Fleet. The hum of the ship's engines starting up was a comforting sound, a promise of their imminent departure. "Secure the technology and run final checks," Ford ordered, his voice steady and authoritative. He felt a sense of pride in his team's accomplishments, but also an underlying tension, knowing they weren't out of danger yet.

Ford moved through the ship, checking in with each crew member. Ria was overseeing the stowing of the valuable tech modules they had retrieved, her eyes alight with excitement. Sam was ensuring the medical supplies were in order, ready for any last-minute emergencies. Jess coordinated the crew, her tactical mind ensuring that everyone was in their assigned positions. "We're almost there," Ford thought, a mix of relief and vigilance in his mind.

Just as the crew began powering up the Galileo's engines, alarms blared through the ship. "Incoming hostiles!" Lana's voice crackled over the intercom. Captain Ford's eyes narrowed as he turned toward the main view port, where Lieutenant Kane and his mercenaries were advancing rapidly. "This isn't over, Ford!" Kane shouted, his voice dripping with cold determination. His operatives fanned out, weapons at the ready, aiming to seize the technology at the last moment.

Captain Graves watched the chaos unfold from a distance, her eyes narrowing as she observed the bravery and determination of Ford's crew. In a decisive moment, she raised her hand and signaled to her mercenaries. "Stand down, men! We're fighting with them now," she commanded, her voice strong and unwavering. Her team hesitated only for a second before moving to support the Galileo's crew, their weapons turning on Kane's forces.

With Graves and her mercenaries now fighting alongside them, the combined forces of the **Galileo** and Graves's team launched a coordinated counterattack. Captain Ford, at the forefront, directed his crew with precision. "Ace, cover the left flank! Jess, hold the center!" he commanded. Blaster fire filled the air as Ford and Graves fought side by side, their efforts synchronized. The relentless push of their unified front began to overwhelm Kane's operatives.

After the last of Kane's operatives had been subdued, Captain Ford and Captain Graves surveyed the battlefield, their expressions grim but satisfied. Ford extended a hand to Graves, a gesture of gratitude and respect. "We couldn't have done it without you," he admitted, his voice sincere. Graves nodded, her grip firm as she shook his hand. "You've earned our respect, Ford. For now, we stand together," she replied, her tone carrying a newfound respect.

✦✦✦

Captain Nathaniel Ford stood on the bridge of the Galileo, sur-
veying the damage from the recent battle. The once pristine control panels were now scorched, and sparks flew intermittently
from exposed wiring. Despite the chaos, the ship remained
functional. "We need a full assessment of the damage," Ford
ordered, his voice calm and authoritative. He watched as his
crew moved with a sense of purpose, their exhaustion clear but
their resolve unwavering.

The crew swiftly divided into teams, each member taking on
specific repair tasks. Ria Lopez focused on the damaged engines,
her hands moving with practiced precision as she diagnosed and
repaired the malfunctioning systems. "I need more coolant over
here!" she called out, and Jess Hayes, overseeing the hull repairs,
relayed the request efficiently. "On it, Ria. Make sure the power
grid is stable," Jess responded, her tactical mind ensuring every
detail was covered.

As they worked together, Ria and Jess's collaboration reflected
a growing mutual respect. They communicated seamlessly, each
recognizing the other's expertise and value to the team. The
synchronized efforts of the entire crew began to bring the Galileo
back to operational status, their coordinated actions a testament
to their unity and determination.

Captain Ford moved through the ship, checking on each team
and their progress. He paused by Ace Morgan, who was working
on stabilizing the navigation systems. "Ace, your quick thinking
during the battle made all the difference," Ford said, clapping
him on the shoulder. Ace grinned, a flicker of pride in his eyes.

Ford then approached Dr. Sam Patel, who was tending to
minor injuries sustained during the repairs. "Sam, your medical
skills kept us going. We couldn't have made it without you,"
Ford acknowledged. Sam nodded, a humble smile on his face.

"Just doing my part, Captain," he replied. Ford's words were sincere, recognizing the strengths and efforts of each crew member, reinforcing the bond they shared.

As repairs continued, Jess and Ria found themselves working side by side on a particularly stubborn power conduit. "I have to admit, your engineering skills are impressive," Jess said, her tone sincere. Ria looked up from her work, a smile spreading across her face. "Thanks, Jess. And I've learned a lot from watching you handle the tactical side of things. We make a pretty good team."

Ace and Sam worked together on the navigation systems, sharing a moment of camaraderie. "You know, Sam, I think we might make a cautious guy out of you yet," Ace joked, glancing at the doctor with a grin. Sam chuckled, shaking his head. "And maybe you'll learn to take a few more calculated risks. Balance is key, after all."

As the repairs neared completion, Captain Ford gathered the crew in the common area. The ship was still a bit rough around the edges, but the worst of the damage had been addressed. "We faced incredible odds and came through because of each one of you," Ford said, his voice filled with pride and gratitude. "Ria, your technical expertise; Sam, your unwavering support; Lana, your brilliance; Jess, your tactical mind; and Ace, your daring spirit. We are stronger together, and today we proved it."

$$***$$

Captain Nathaniel Ford stood at the head of a large conference table in a bustling space station, the Galileo safely docked nearby. Around him, his crew members sat, their expressions a mix of pride and anticipation. Representatives from various sectors of the galactic community filled the room, their eyes fixed on Ford. "We've made incredible discoveries, and it's time to share them," Ford began, his voice steady and confident. He glanced at his crew, each one ready to present their findings.

As Ford continued to speak, he introduced each crew member to the audience. Ria Lopez stood first, displaying holographic images of the advanced technology they had retrieved. Dr. Sam Patel followed, discussing the potential medical advancements derived from their findings. Jess Hayes provided a detailed analysis of the tactical insights they had gained, while Ace Morgan shared crucial navigation data. The representatives listened intently, their expressions shifting from curiosity to admiration. The atmosphere in the room was charged with excitement and respect.

As each crew member presented their findings, Captain Ford watched the audience's reactions. Ria's detailed explanations of the advanced technology had several representatives nodding in approval, while Sam's discussion on potential medical breakthroughs drew murmurs of excitement. Jess's tactical insights were met with keen interest, and Ace's navigation data earned appreciative nods. "Your contributions will greatly benefit the entire galaxy," one official remarked, stepping forward to shake Ford's hand.

As the meeting concluded, Captain Ford stepped back, allowing his crew to bask in the recognition they had earned. He watched as the representatives mingled with his team, offering congratulations and asking questions. Ford felt a deep sense of pride swell within him. They had faced overwhelming odds and emerged stronger. The dangers of the Forsaken Fleet, the battles, the alliances—all of it had led to this moment. "We've come a long way," he thought, his gratitude for his crew's unity and resilience palpable.

Lana Mitchell stepped up to the podium, her composed de-meanor drawing the attention of the room. "Our mission was a testament to what we can achieve when we work together," she began, her voice clear and articulate. "The discoveries we made are not just about technology or knowledge—they're about the resilience and spirit of humanity. We succeeded because we were united, facing every challenge together."

As Lana finished her speech, the room erupted in applause. The crew of the Galileo stepped off the podium, met with warm congratulations and heartfelt thanks from the representatives. Captain Ford watched his team, seeing the pride and joy on their faces. "We did it," he said quietly to himself, a sense of fulfillment washing over him. The recognition and respect they received solidified their status as heroes, embodying the indomitable spirit of humanity.

About the Author

You can connect with me on:

🌐 https://www.youtube.com/@BoneSpears-and-StarShips

Also by Bone Spears and StarShips